THE ALL NEW STYLE OF MAGAZINE-BOOKS

SDM LIVE®

www.SDMLIVE.com

MP

MOCY PUBLISHING
WWW.MOCYPUBLISHING.COM

Printed by CreateSpace, An Amazon.com Company

SDM LIVE®

EDITOR-IN-CHIEF
D. "Casino" Bailey
casino@sdmlive.com

EDITORIAL DIRECTOR
Sheree Cranford
sheree@sdmlive.com

GRAPHIC/WEB DESIGNER
D. "Casino" Bailey
casino@sdmlive.com

ACCOUNT EXECUTIVE
Frank Harvest Jr.
frank@sdmlive.com

PHOTOGRAPHERS
Anterlon Terrell Fritz
Treagen Colston
Terance Drake

CONTRIBUTORS
April Smiley
Courtney Benjamin

COPY ORDERS & ADVERTISING OFFICE
Send Money Order or Check to:
Mocy Publishing
P.O. Box 35195
Detroit, Michigan 48235
(586) 646-8505
advertise@sdmlive.com

Copy Order Item #12

SDM Live Magazine Issue #12 2017
S&H Plus Retail Price - $9.99 per copy

WWW.SDMLIVE.COM

Printed by CreateSpace, An Amazon.com Company

REAL MUSIC. REAL ENTERTAINMENT.®
SDM LIVE
ISSUE 12

Also
PHILLY FAL
7MILE
RADIO
NO'EL
SNYDER
SARAH
APPLEB
LASURIA
"KANDI"
ALLMAN

NEW
KING DILLON
EXCLUSIVE P DOT

CHARLIE B. KEYZ
PUTTING IN MAJOR
LEGWORK IN THE
INDUSTRY

TOYSOULJA
LAGOON
THE NEWEST
MEMBER OF
TEAM MONEY
HUNGRY

WWW.SDMLIVE.COM

ISSUE 12 - 2017

CONTENTS

1

Nikon - D3400 DSLR Camera with AF-P DX 18-55mm G VR and 70-300mm G ED Lenses - Black
$599.99
www.bestbuy.com

2

Lorex - 4-Channel, 4-Camera Outdoor Wireless 1080p 1TB DVR Surveillance System - White
$499.99
www.bestbuy.com

3

Garmin - vivomove Sport Activity Tracker - Black
$102.99
www.bestbuy.com

SDM^{LIVE}RADIO®

DOWNLOAD THE SDM LIVE APP AT WWW.SDMLIVE.COM

Trigga Don't Do It

VA LEGEND TREY SONGZ GOES FROM MR. STEAL YOUR GIRL TO MR. MUGSHOT AFTER AN ENRAGED PERFORMANCE AT THE JOE

by Cheraee C.

The last big music event in Detroit, Michigan of 2016 was the Big Show at the Joe. The lineup included Chris Brown, Neisha Neshae, Young M.A., Lil Yachty, Desiigner, Icewear Vezzo, Zay Hilfiger, Zay McCall, and Trey Songz. With such a big lineup and some additional performers added to the show, performance times were limited. Every artist was given a time slot, but sometimes 10 seconds of fame is not enough.

R&B star Trey Songz was feeling himself when he was performing in font of Detroit. His performance time was over, but he refused to drop the mic. Trey was forewarned by Joe Louis set managers that if he didn't leave the stage when his time was up, his mic would be cut off. Maybe he was never threatend to have his mic cut off before. In response, Trey dared Joe Louis officials to cut his mic off and harmo-nized to the audience. Trey told Detroit if his mic was cut off he would go ludicrous and act a fool. Without bluffing, Trey's mic was shut off and outraged he began wilding out. He was allegedly tearing up the stage, throwing speakers, microphones, and grabbed anything in sight and reach. His rage allegedly caused him to injure a police officer and landed him a night in jail in Dickerson. He was charged with assault on a police officer causing injury and misdemeanor aggravated assault.

I think Trey Songz saw an opportunity to do a publicity stunt and he did. He wanted to end 2016 with a bang, increase his ratings, and let his fans see a side of Trey they've never seen. Just yesterday he was singing about how the neighbors know his name, now he got a mugshot singing f*** the police. Boy, do artists change quickly and the images they paint for the world to see.

The Art of Deviancy

CHERAEE C. TAKES A SEXY LEAP INTO THE DARK SIDE WITH THE EROTIC MINDFRAMES OF SEXUALLY, DEVIANT COUNTERPARTS

by Cheraee C.

To be deviant is to be wild, free, promscious, and differ from the expected and usual norms and standards of the modern, traditional, and basic society. It's a lot of deviant women and men in the world with numerous sexual drives, economic climaxes, and relationship statuses. Cheraee C. tackles the deviant mind, body, and spirit in her latest thrill-seeker Deviancy. I Love The Thrill. Cheraee C. switches highs and lows with moments of pleasure and moments of pain.

The main character Infiniti Brooks is an unstoppable, highly respectable, kinky woman whom every woman having static in their love life wants to be. Like they say if you can't beat them, join them. This book is a goodread and will soon have a continuation.

**Deviancy:
I Love The Thrill**
By Cheraee C.

Available from Amazon.com and other online stores

Return of The King

THE DIRTBOY KING IS TIGHTENING UP ALL HIS CORNERS AND AVENUES WITH NEW PERCEPTIONS, NEW STRATEGIES, AND NEW MANAGEMENT

By: Cheraee C.

Q. What's been going on with King Dillon during these last six months?

A. I've just been working nonstop in the studio putting countless hours into writing and creating ideas that will help my brand and name as an artist. I been a little under the radar so it may seem like I've been hiding, but beasts never hide in caves, they eat there.

Q. Everybody has new year resolutions. What are some you made for yourself for 2K17?

A. A new year doesn't mean there will be a new me, but it is a new start to do things better than I did and make better decisions. I just plan to stay more focus on myself and growing as an individual. Me going through life is what makes my music. Good vibes = good music.

Q. Focus is key, so what/who do you think the success blockers been in your career?

A. My road to success has been blocked by my mistakes, people I've lost close to me, bad relationships, and fake friends all bullshit. I learned to watch out for BS and everybody on it. The more I let the negative around, the more baggage came with the trip. I had to let all that go and stay focused because when I reach my goal I wanna feel like I made the best decision for me and my career the smart way. Those people will then realize how nothing stopped me from completing the mission.

Q. What's your take on relationships... Is it better to be in the industry first?

A. Knowing what I know now, I think it's more easier to manage your career if you are single. Being in a relationship means two people count for everything. You then have to make more sacrifices than you usually would by yourself.

Q. How do you plan to brand yourself this year? Any sponsorships, clothing lines, motion pictures or etc in the works?

A. Branding myself this year, I'll be promoting more of KD. I'll show my face more, drop new visuals, start my clothing line, and also make an appearance on national television. That's my word. I want the world to finally know who Dillon is and accept my brand, and embrace my artistry.

7 Mile, Better Mile

THE REALEST INTERNET BROADCAST MEDIA OUTLET IN THE CITY'S LIMITS:
7 MILE RADIO BEEN KILLING RADIO WAVES SINCE 2007
by Cheraee C.

Q. Who started 7 Mile Radio and out of all the local miles in Michigan why was it named after 7 Mile?

A. 7 Mile Radio was founded in 2007 by Marc D as a practice studio for the creation of demo radio shows for him to take to major stations in hopes of getting a job. It morphed into a platform for local Hip Hop artists and artists across genres. Since Marc D is from the 7 Mile area he decided that would be a signature way to identify his company as a Detroit entity without using the connection to the 8 Mile movie and brand that was popular at that time.

Q. What type of radio station is 7 Mile Radio and what shows does 7 Mile Radio headline?

A. 7 Mile Radio is an award-winning digital media resource and internet broadcast company generating in Detroit, Michigan. 7 Mile Radio highlights independent concept based radio content like Marc D's Open House Live Show airing Mondays, Wednesdays, Fridays, and some Sundays at 1pm and 7pm. Also, it includes 7 Mile Radio's longest running show, Back on the B Cyde airing Saturdays at 11am hosted by Tracie "T Elice" Chrisitan. The station has been home to shows ranging in subject matter from books, food reviews, and relationships to current affairs, gospel, and local/national entertainment news.

Q. Who is Tracie "T Elice" Christian and how has she advanced being with 7 Mile Radio?

A. She is a former interviewee that stayed with the company after her author's interview and worked her way up the ladder from Studio Trainee, to On-Air personality, to show host/engineer, to producer/station manager, and to now co-owner since 2009.

Q. What is the most memorable interview that 7 Mile Radio has ever did and why?

A. Marc D- My most memorable interview was with Dick Gregory because of the insight and wisdom I gained from that sitdown conversation. "I love to interview people that make me re-evaluate how I look at the world."

T Elice- My most memorable interview to date was with Eric Nolan of the legendary R&B group The O'Jays because he was so down to earth and honest. "It wasn't like I was talking with a celebrity who was untouchable, it was two music lovers discussing the statee of the music in his day and age. It was the coolest moment."

Q. Compared to other radio stations/internet based radio stations, what's different about 7 Mile Radio?

A. Well the most obvious difference between 7 Mile Radio and the rest is the fact that we operate out of two separate studios. Marc D has Studio A Media Outlet for news and Hip Hop and T Elice separates The B Cyde Studio for books, poetry, and R&B/Soul division of 7 Mile Radio. Another difference is that we offer services beyond our radio broadcast component. We offer on-location event coverage, audio, and video promotion/production, graphic arts, music videos, merchandise, audio book narration services and more. We pride ourselves in staying in touch with the advancements in technology to offer a one-of-a kind experience.

Music is Power

FREELANCE WRITER AND MUSIC REVIEWER NO'EL SNYDER SHARES HIS LOVE
FOR MUSIC AND THE PATH HE CHOSE IN THE MUSIC INDUSTRY
by: Cheraee C.

Q. What led to your deep love for music?

A. Music is such a beautiful art form. No matter what mood you're in, there's a song to match your emotion. I grew up listening to Next, Color Me Bad, @pac, and Aaliyah so coming from that, I found myself listening to catch my favorite lyric or what stood out to me the most in the song and it just grew from there.

Q. What drove you to start writing music reviews?

A. I told myself 7 years ago that I would meet the music artists that I listen to on a daily basis. I wanted to connect with these artists on a personal level because I can relate to their lyrics. I wanted to meet the people who influenced me the most musically, and I figured if I enjoy music as much as I do, then why not write about it. I want others to relate to what I hear, and how certain songs stimulate my mind and body. I wnt to put people hip to good music because I know what good music sounds like. I can alter someone's entire perception on a certain song or artist just by giving someone a more in depth meaning behind the melody. I'm very good at catching references within the music and just listening to the lyrics, because being able to annotate them is a blessing.

Q. How did you end up being a writer for JetLag TV and what type of Detroit artists have you done music reviews on?

A. I was contacted and congradulated at the same time by the owner of JetLag TV. He said he liked my reviews, and he ran a website similar to Complex or XXL and he wanted more people like me on his team. I contacted him and took him up on his offer. I interviewed a lot of very talented people who have great potential.

Q. If you could write for any magazine in the U.S. who would you write for and why?

A. Awh, there are so many amazing magazines that cover music, but if I had to choose, it would be XXL Magazine. With XXL Magazine turning 20 htis year, that alone just shows the dedication and history within the company, covering music since the late 90's. Such a trusted source for music,

so it's something I'd like to be involved with. To see my name in that magazine covering music reviews one day, you never know.... but I'm happy and I'm grateful where I ended up. Just enjoying the ride and living in the moment.

Q. At what point of writing did you seek management and how do you feel about your current manager?

A. In the beginning I never sought management. I was always the type to get things done on my own. Doing my own promotion/advertisement, setting mettings, and attending shows. Just giving my support at every event. But as my career and life progresses, it gets difficult to prioritize time with life. Start to dwell on which is more important. So it's great having someone who can take care of those tasks for me. Thank God I have such a productive and positive manager. S/O to Kizzy Snyder.

Pushing Her Pen

IN 2017 RAP STAR P DOT IS REDEFINING HER BRAND WITH NEW MANAGEMENT AS AN INDEPENDENT FEMCEE, AN ACTRESS, AND A PERFORMER

by Cheraee C.

Q. What's been going on in the world of PDot since your last interview with SDM?

A. I've made a lot of progress. Shows are more frequent and stages have gotten bigger. I've won best female Hip-Hop artist of the year with both the Detroit Black Music Awards and Detroit Honor Awards. I've also been nominated and made Top 5 for best female Hip-Hop artist of the Year and best live performer with the Underground Hip Hop Awards. I have a couple of movie roles in What People Do For Money, My Street Life and Something Shady web series. So things are picking up and looking bright. I'm very thankful and grateful.

Q. Branding is important and you've started showing us the sexy, feminine side of you slaying red carpets, stages, and photo shoots. What motivated you and why did you decide to soften up a bit and give us sexy?

A. Because I feel like with everything there's growth. Nothing remains the same. I want to be the femcee that brings class back to Hip-Hop like it should be. I don't want to ever be put into a box. I want to represent the ordinary woman. I've evolved and it's time to show it.

Q. Females are constantly being used, shortchanged, and exploited in the music industry. Has your brand experienced any of these negative challenges?

A. I've managed to dodge that bullet. Being that I am a god-fearing woman, I always pray and ask God to grant me the discernment. I have always been able to feel and recognize when people are approaching me with bad intentions or agendas. I've always wanted to just "be myself" and that has actually worked for me.

Q. You have a huge fan-base who got your back like the Beehive, but it's the P-hive. Why do you think your fans are so protective, cutthorat, and diligent towards you?

A. I don't know but, I appreciate it. One of my supporters, I hate to use the word fans, told me they had been following me and rooting for me since I was in high school. I guess they really love me and I love them too.

Q. 2017 is the year of execution, how do you plan on executing your goals this year?

A. By keeping God 1st and following his lead. By remaining true to self and following my heart and my passion which is my music.

No Room For Leeches

INDIE ARTIST SARAH APPLEB ELABORATES ON BEING A SOLO ARTIST, BEING IN A MUSIC GROUP, AND THE MISCONCEPTIONS OF BEING A FEMALE ARTIST

by Cheraee C.

Q. How do you choose the artists, producers, promoters etc that you work with? What are your industry deal breakers as an artist?

A. I usually watch the way someone move through social media and get references when it comes to choosing because these days I'm more focused on doing business the right way. As an artist, I need to be able to create the things I want to the way I want and that is a deal breaker for me when it comes to the music industry.

Q. Describe your first experience in a recording studio?

A. I was still in high school when I first recorded at a studio. The feeling was like no other. I never looked back after that and after hearing myself over the beat really took over me.

Q. Tell us about the female duo Beautiful Bosses. Who started the duo, who's in the duo, and what's the current status of the duo?

A. Beautiful Bosses was started by myself and label-mate Kitty Kash. Right now our focus is on building our brand and releasing another joint project.

Q. What are 3 misconceptions about female artists you would like to change in the game?

A. One misconception I feel is its not all about the look listen to the lyrics. I feel we have to pass a phsycial test first with most listeners hence the reason i feel a lot of females are doing more plastic surgery. Another thing is we ae not all overly sexy. I like to make music about real topics and some type of message behind it. I also want people to see that you can be CEO of your own label and do things on your own. I know a lot of females who wait on somebody else to push them and its nothing, but a hold up.

Q. Who is Sarah behind the music and how are your 24 hours and 7 days a week spent?

A. Behind the music I'm just a laid back, down to earth chick that spends most of my free time at home with my family. Most of my day consists of taking care of my 2 lil boys, reading, and writing. I'm in transition mode right now. I started my own label almost a year ago so now I"m in between building my brand and balancing my personal life.

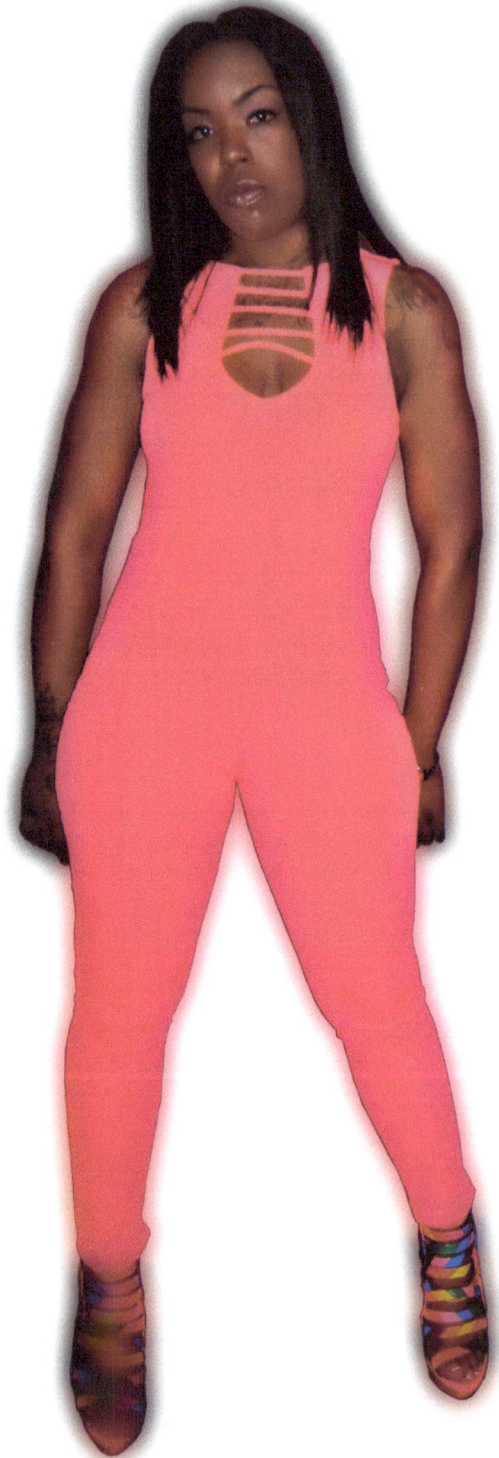

Chart Toppers of 2017

BILLBOARD'S TOP 10 RANKED R&B/HIP HOP ARTISTS RISING IN 2017

by Semaja Turner

A lot of artists produced major keys in the music industry for 2016, and are expected to be the best of 2017. Between music streams, songwriting credits, chart ratings, and mainstream industry affliations, these artists have proved their worth and their talents are fundamental to the music industry.

Since the industry is ever-changing and never stops, these upcoming artists better land their AMA's, their Grammy's, and get their platinum record statuses while they are in the hot seat.

1. Kehlani
2. Amine
3. YFN Lucci
4. Leela James
5. Kodie Shane
6. Princess Nokia
7. Guordan Banks
8. Tekno
9. Khalid
10. H.E.R.

Learn Your Craft

VOCALIST CHARLIE B. KEYZ HAS PUT MAJOR LEGWORK IN THE
INDUSTRY THROUGH SCHOOLING, INTERNING, AND NETWORKING

by Cheraee C.

Q. A lot of artists don't study their crafts by the book so what led
you so what led you to study music theory and music composi-
tion? And is their any other music expertise that you have from
school, trades, lessons, etc?

A. Music has always been something important to meas well as
learning everything I can to be the best at it. Going to school
seemed right although my path is completely different from
where I started. Learning music and being apart of everything it
encompasses completes me. By learning the piano, guitar, violin,
choral arrangement understanding, chord progressions, and being able to compose, etc. School definitely helped my sound.

Q.. Tell us about the first feature you did with an artist from
when it occurred, what artist you worked with, how it was ar-
ranged, and the name of the song?

A. My first feature was with an artist Antonia @toniamusic
accompanied the track with piano. It's called No Sleep and this
was one of many great experiences that I've been apart of and
she is such a phonominal vocalist. She asked if I could come
in after a show we where apart of together and played with the
concept and it was awesome. The chemistry and the feeling was
amazing. I've also done a feature with JP One and working on a
few others. As I interned with Sony and Atlantic Records I had
many opportunities working behind the scenes of a few mainstream artists alongside a team of others.

Q. How and when did you intern at Sony and Atlantic Records?
What mainstream artists did you work with there?

A. I worked as an intern for Sony and Atlantic Records from
2010 til mid 2011. It was through a program with my curricu-
lum at Florida State. We did work behind Livvi Frank and also
Chrisette Michelle when she was assisting with co-writing and
working with Sony Music Entertainment. Also this group called
Destine I believe they where an alternative rock group.

Q. What is the biggest challenge you've faced in dealing with
people in the musicindustry?

A. There's a saying, "there are many chefs and not Indians"
because of this the challenge for me is finding and knowing that
there are many talented and amazing artists and giuring out
how to place the pieces together to make a great project is not
always an easy task. Scheduling and effort also play a big role in
an effective and great project.

Q. What do you do in your spare time when your not doing
music?

A. My life is mostly centered on music mostly so listening to
other artists and being inspired by others to create is a great
feeling. When I am away from creating music I'm spending time
working on how to stay focused, how to build a brand that
inspires people to do positive things. Also creating avenues
for positive growth in my community to help guide people to
put forth the effort to do what they want to do in life.

Q. What is the most exciting thing up next for you whether it
be a mixtape, album release, single release, show, or etc?

A. My EP Portrait I'm excited to complete this project because it's a direct reflection of myself and my life. I'm hoping
that it will inspire others and give people insight of who I am
as not only an artist, but as a person. We all have different
paths, situations, and life change-ups and this EP is not only a
segway into the album after, but a way of letting people know
you also have the opportunity to grow within yourself and do
what you need to become much more than where in life you
are now.

Turning Pages into Money

AUTHOR LASURIA "KANDI" ALLMAN TURNED HER HIT NOVEL "WHAT PEOPLE DO FOR MONEY" INTO A CROWD PLEASER COMING TO THE BIG SCREEN

by Cheraee C.

Q. What made you turn your book What People Do For Money into a movie?

A. My readers kept asking for Part 2 so I decided to start writing Part 2. Then I got a call from Maniyac saying he was ready to film "What People Do For Money." I just had left Detroit touring and promoting for four months. I was back home 26 days when I received the call. I flew out to Detroit 5 days later to start filming.

Q. How'd you begin working with Maniyac and why'd you pick him to be your movie's producer?

A. Maniyac and I have known each other since 2009. I love his work, and he is very good at capturing the moment getting that money shot. He is also a very great editor so I knew it wold be a perfect match. He knew that I have tons of material to film. Right now we can film 45 movies and be tied up doing 5 movies a year for the next 9 years. I have so many books and scripts.

Q. Can you summarize the movie's plot?

A. Growing up on the streets of Detroit struggling to surive their lives changed when Honey met FATS. He is a big time drug dealer who took over the westside territory and developed beef in the streets. While FATS was away on business, Honey was savagely raped and robbed in their home. That is when all hell breaks loose and FATS starts a war with everyone. No one was safe and his goons terrorized an entire community. This is a story about drugs, pimps, whores, hustlers, drug dealers, players, sex, and lies. Friendships are betrayed and each character has their own story and Karma. This story will have you on the edge of your seat begging for more.

Q. Did you stick to the plot and dialogue of your book as you created your movie script and were filming?

A. No and yes... I wanted to bring each character to life. Also, I added a few additional roles to spice it up more.

Q. How many books have you written and how long have you been writing and publishing books?

A. I've written 26 books and published 8 for others. Actually you will be surprised I wrote my first book "Her Stolen Pride" in October 2013 about my mother who is civil rights activist Mamie King-Chalmers.

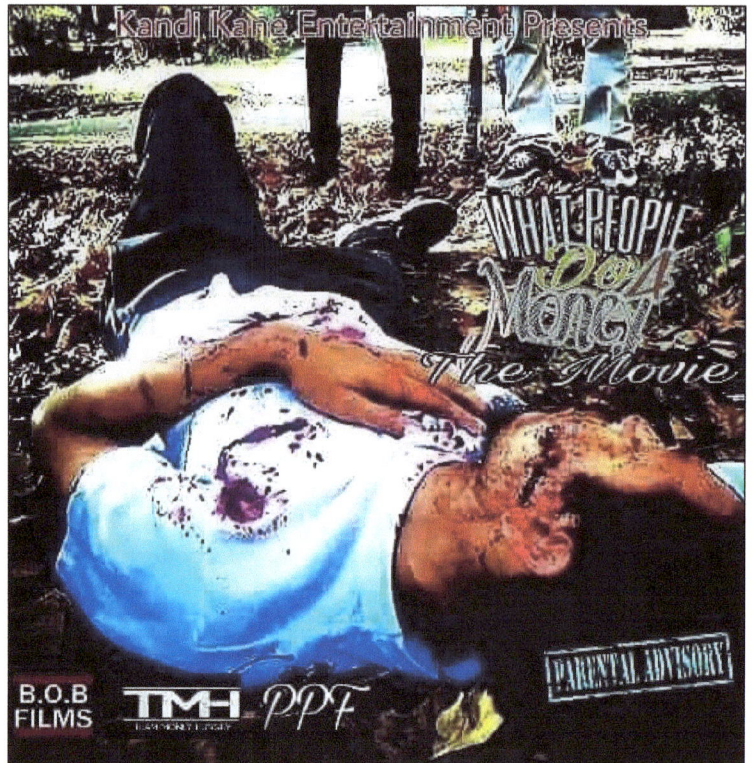

Q. Besides being an author, what other skills and titles do you have?

A. I am the CEO of Kandi Kane ENT which consists of Kandi Kane Radio which I have 4 shows on including The Network, The Hot Seat, The Hot Seat Underground, Takin it to the Streets and Allies of the Throne. I own Kandi Kane Movies, I'm a movie producer, Kandi Kane Publishing, I'm PR for my mother, I do The Hot Seat Underground Magazine, I am the manager of Get Wit It Records, and an author.

Q. When and where can fans expect to see What People Do For Money on a movie screen?

A. What People Do For Money will be released in March. Go to YouTube and watch the What People Do For Money movie trailer.

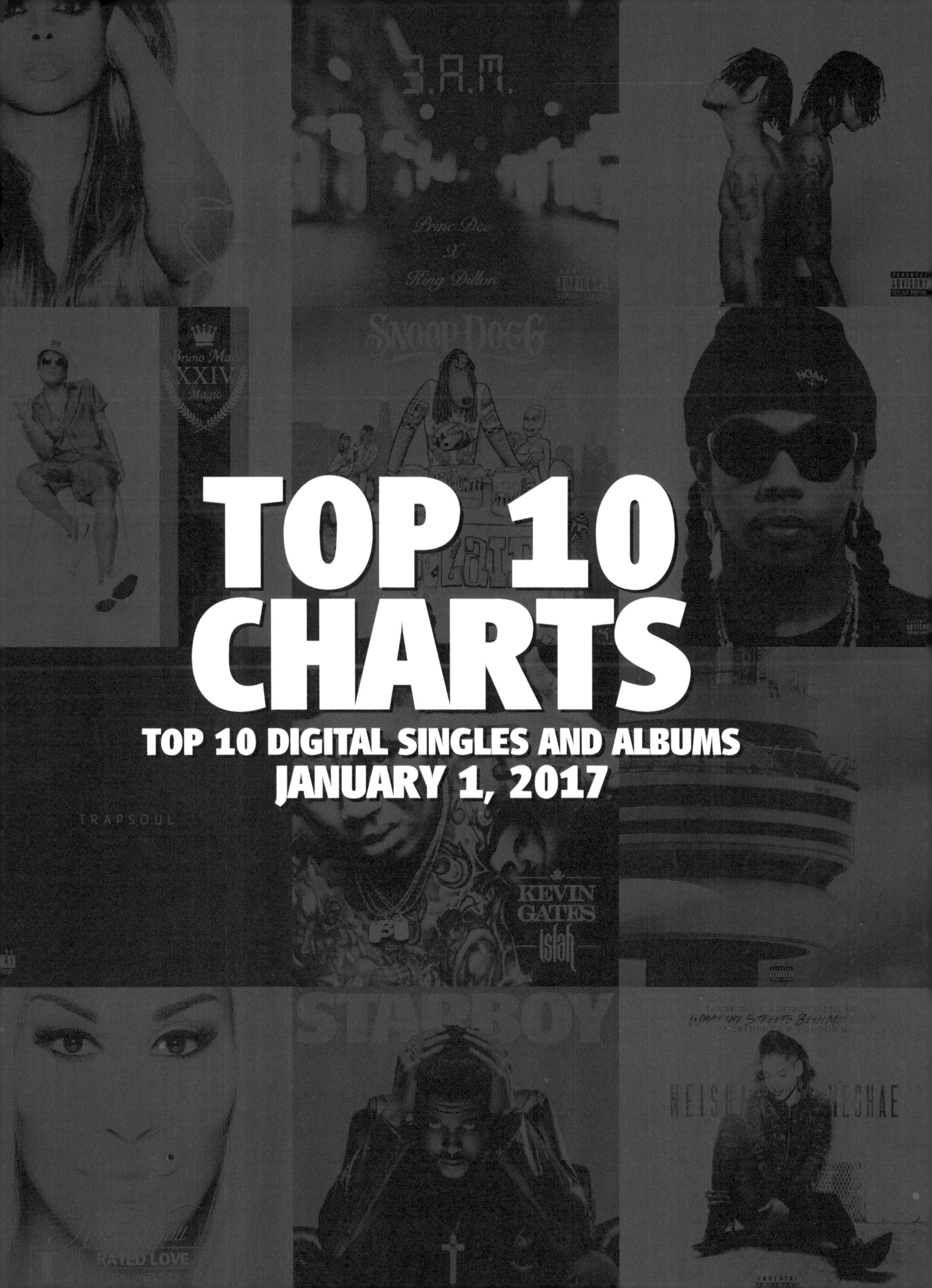

TOP 10 CHARTS

TOP 10 DIGITAL SINGLES AND ALBUMS
JANUARY 1, 2017

TOP 10 CHARTS

TOP #1

RAPPER GROUP RAE SREMMURD HITS RADIO.COM WITH AN EXCLUSIVE INTERVIEW.

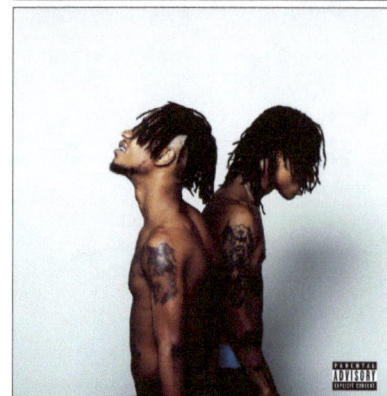

Rae Sremmurd
Black Beatles
*Coming in at #1 this month,
The mannequin challenge
theme song continues to be
a real crowd pleaser.*

TOP 10 SINGLES
CHART OF THE MONTH

No.	Artist - Song Title
1	RAE SREMMURD - BLACK BEATLES
2	BRUNO MARS - 24K MAGIC
3	ZAY HILFIGERRR & ZAYLON MCCALL - JUJU ON THAT BEAT
4	MACHINE GUN KELLY - BAD THINGS
5	DRAKE - FAKE LOVE
6	MIGOS - BAD AND BOUJEE
7	YOUNG M.A. - OOOUUU
8	RIHANNA - LOVE ON THE BRAIN
9	BIG SEAN - BOUNCE BACK
10	J. COLE - DEJA VU

TOP 10 ALBUMS
CHART OF THE MONTH

No.	Artist - Album Title
1	BRUNO MARS - 24K MAGIC
2	THE WEEKND - STARBOY
3	KEKE WYATT - RATED LOVE
4	A TRIBE CALLED QUEST - WE GOT IT FROM HERE... THANK YOU FOR 4 SERVICE
5	THE LOX - FILTHY AMERICA... IT'S BEAUTIFUL
6	GUCCI MANE - THE RETURN OF EAST ATLANTA SANTA
7	YO GOTTI - WHITE FRIDAY (CM9)
8	TI - US OR ELSE (EP)
9	RAE SREMMURD - SREMMLIFE 2
10	LIL UZI VERT - LIL UZI VERT VS. THE WORLD

24K Magic

ARTIST: Bruno Mars
REVIEWER: Cheraee C.
RATING: 4

After listening to this Bruno Mars' album I realized he is an incredible artist that's not to be slept on. Bruno has a new school mixed with a old school flow. His album only has nine tracks and no features, yet it's #1 on the Billboards.

Tracks you'll blast through the city include the hit single 24K Magic, That's What I Like, Perm, Chunky, Versace On The Floor, Calling All My Lovelies, Finesse, Straight Up and Down, and a few other blazing tracks. I give this album four stars.

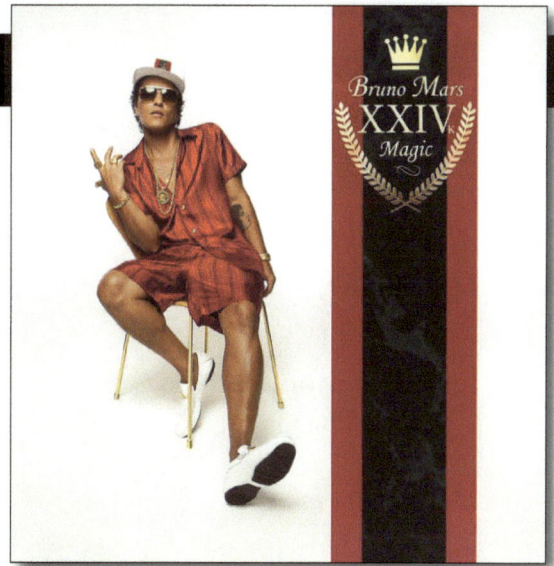

RATE METER: 1 - WACK   2 - NEEDS WORK   3 - STRAIGHT   4 - BANGER   5 - CLASSIC

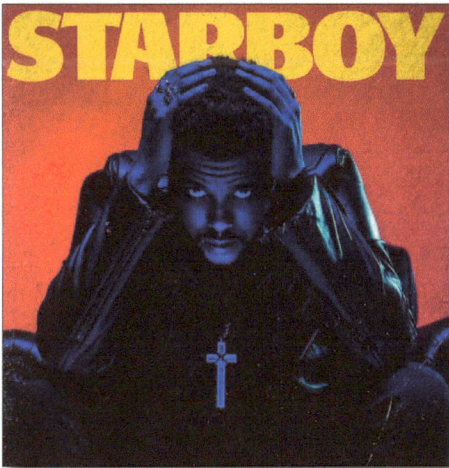

Starboy

ARTIST: The Weeknd
REVIEWER: Cheraee C.
RATING: 5

Canadian singer and songwriter The Weeknd is on the third chapter of his music. He continues to serve the music world with versatility, origniality, and realism. Guest appearances on this project include Daft Punk, Lana Del Rey, Future, and Kendrick Lamar. The top 3 singles in this album include "Starboy", "I Feel it Coming," and "Party Monster." I give his album five stars.

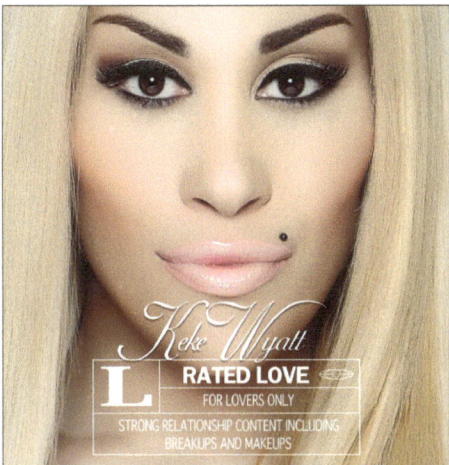

Rated Love

ARTIST: Keke Wyatt
REVIEWER: Cheraee C.
RATING: 2

The Atlanta R&B diva Keke Wyatt is in full comeback mode as she releases her fourth project. The best song on the album is her radio and YouTube hit "Jodeci." Besides, that song the other tracks are depressing and gloomy. Maybe as she was recording this album she was going through dark times. I give the album the 2 stars.

HEELS & SKILLZ

Kayla McNeal
is a beautiful model
from Detroit, MI.

instagram
@blondiee_

Photography by
Terance Drake

HEELS & SKILLZ

Bigsexz

Founder and C.E.O. of Bigsexz from the D Calendar and Print model and Motivator who loves to inspire.

instagram
@bigsexz4real

Photography by
Terance Drake

HEELS & SKILLZ

Nona

is a sexy model
for barearmy and
lives in Detroit, MI.

instagram
nonamalone313

*Photography by
@barearmy*

Cheraee's Corner
WHAT IS THE DEFINITION AND REAL MEANING OF UNDERGROUND HIP HOP?
by Cheraee C.

There is a world of Hip-Hop in the mecca of the streets and I call it the underworld of Hip-Hop where underground artists flourish and triumph. What does it mean to be an underground artist? Underground artists are unsigned, undiscovered, underrated, and street-publicized artists. They are always headlining at local shows, showcases, and concerts in which the majority of local events and activities are self-made, self-promoted, and self-orgaanized. Underground artists live their music by constantly releasing singles, mixtapes, EP's, LP's, joint projects, and freestyles or etc. The underground nation releases their music on YouTube, iTunes, Audiosmack, SoundCloud, ReverbNation, and other digital outlets aimed at more exposure and instant avaliability.

The only reason why the underground world is currently suffering and divided is because people don't understand what underground is, what loyalty is, or what good business is.

Most importantly underground artists represent themselves, fund themselves, and they need love too as well as underground music. Underground artists do not get enough love and support in their cities, at award ceremonies designed to award underground music, or by local radio stations, local DJ's, or local producers who claim to be representers and leaders of the underground world. Some Detroit underground artists include JP One. King Dillion, Team Money Hungry, Black Lion Society, PDot, Gucci Rie, and it's a thousand others.

NEXT 2 BLOW

TOYSOULJA LAGOON

Q. A lot of female MC's lack consistency and longevity. Is music something you plan to do forever or until you hit a certain age, net worth, or mindframe?

A. I have always had a passion for writing music so I don't believe that I will ever stop so yes I plan on doing music until I can't anymore.

Q. Artists face obstacles everyday. What obstacles in your life do you think might interrupt/interfere with your music career?

A. My music career is priority over almost everything in my everyday life that is how dedicated I am to it. The only obstacle I can say that I face is the financial support that comes along with being an artist.

Q. There's always stories about artists and venues. Have you performed at over/under 50 venues yet and describe the craziest memoory you have at a venue performance.

A. I would say under 50 venues, but I am very close to the 50 mark. The craziest story I have has got to be the time I was on stage performing my single "Swish" and there was a fight going on by the bar. No one had even noticed because we was all haing fun and the crowd was vibing to my performance. After I was done performing I noticed that my throat started getting a little burning feeling and my eyes were starting to water. I guess someone had used pepper spray in the crowd. The next day I found out it was because of the fight that broke out. I was just amused that I didn't even notice the fight while I was on stage.

Q. Do people ever compare you to any mainstream female MC's and what mainstream female artists do you admire?

A. People usually compare me to Da Brat. The artists I admire are Eminem, Hopsin, Tech N9ne, and Nas.

Q. What is your main focus moving into 2017 and what are some of the do's and don't you're learned in the game?

A. I want to finish my album and grinding as hard as I can. The big don't I have learned is never do business with anyone unless there is paperwork involved. The do(s) are to always network with other artists and keep an open mind.

Q.

Describe some of the obstacles you faced in life before the music industry and now in the industry?

A. Before the music industry, I was faced with many different obstacles. The most significant ones were my father abandoning my five siblings and myself at age 9. Then to be followed by my mother's boyfriend who molested me, shortly after. These two events alone led me to write poetry, which eventually turned to lyricism at age 11. While I am just entering the music industry, music has always been a stress reliever. Now that I am involved in the industry one of the biggest obstacles I face is to trust people. I'm coming to find everything that looks good and sounds is not good.

Q. You play in the upcoming movie What People Do For Money. Describe your role, your experience filming, and if this is your first film.

A. First let me say Lasuria Kandi Allman is a beautiful person and I am honored to be a part of What People Do For Money. This is my first film, my first taste of acting, and I must say I love every minute of it. From meeting all the beautiful spirited people to enjoying the bloopers and even going out to party with the cast. The whole experience has been phenomenal. I play myself "Philly" in the movie. I am Edward's (a drug pin) right hand affiliate. I have moments when I am the hood avenger then moments where I start commotion in the hood. My character is a person who has loyalty to a certain extent, but also has anger and desire to have it all. The question people should really want answered is in the end will "Philly" be friend or foe. Can't wait to March 2017 so everyone can find out.

Q. How did you get the opportunity to be in the movie What People Do For Money?

A. The opportunity arose October 16, 2016. I performed at the Star Life at the Takeover 4 with Kandi Kane Entertainment. Funny way Lasuria and myself were introduced. I actually was upset because they kept pushing my performance time back because they were filming the movie. I had no idea. I just knew all my supporters were leaving so I was about to leave. I told my people let's go and as I as I was walking out Donna Banks came after me. She apologized and introduced me to Lasuria Allman. At the time, I was going off, ranting and raving, and the whole time she just had a blank stare, then responded by saying, "I want you in my movie, I have the perfect role for you." The rest was history our journey had begun.

Q. Are you happy with your music career right now and what plans do you have for your career in the new year?

A. This is going to sound crazy, but it's the truth. While I can make money off of music, it's not my goal to. Most artists make music for their fans, but I make music for myself. Music is my personal therapy I just decided to share with the world. If you like my music let's rock and if you don't, you don't. I think as long as I am able to make music constantly I will always be happy with my music career. My plans for the upcoming year are to perfect my craft and share raw honesty within my music without caring about repercussions. People hide behind fake facades trying to be something they are not. This year will be very controversial and I will show people it's ok to be yourself. No one can do you like you.

PHILLY FAL

SNAP SHOTS

Email Your Snap Shots to
snapshots@sdmlive.com

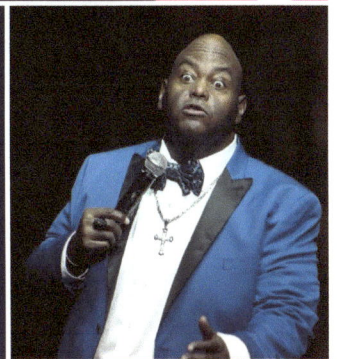

5DS PRODUCTIONS®
THE PRINT MEDIA CENTER.

PRINT

GET 10% OFF WITH CODE: SAVE10OFF

DIGITAL & PRESS RUN PRICE LIST

BUSINESS CARD 2x3.5 INCHES		TRIFOLD BROCHURE 8.5x11 INCHES		POSTCARDS 4x6 INCHES	
100	$10	250	$150	250	$50
500	$20	500	$180	500	$55
1000	$30	1000	$230	1000	$65
5000	$100	5000	$350	5000	$130
10000	$170	10000	$680	10000	$250

**FLYERS - BROCHURES - BANNERS - BUSINESS CARDS - CD INSERTS
CALENDARS - EVENT TICKETS - POSTCARDS - POSTERS
YARD SIGNS - AND MUCH MORE**

DIGITAL & PRESS RUN PRINTING

FAST TURN AROUND PRINTING

GET FREE SHIPPING ON ALL ORDERS

YOU SAVE MONEY WHEN YOU PRINT AT
WWW.THEPRINTMEDIACENTER.COM
24/7 ONLINE ORDERING. CALL US NOW 1.888.718.2999

COUPON CODE IS FOR A LIMITED TIME OFFER - FREE UPS SHIPPING ANYWHERE IN THE US

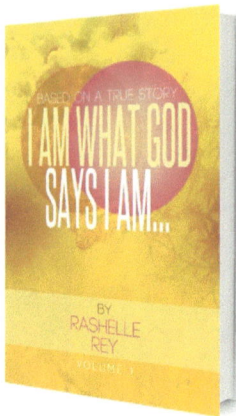

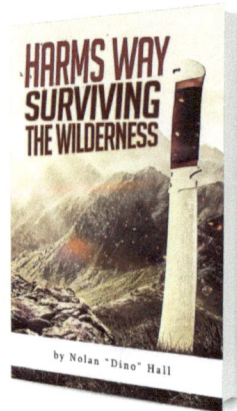

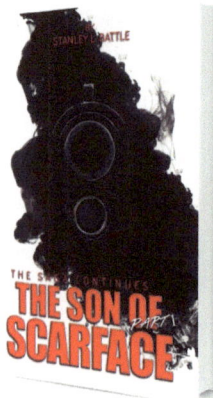

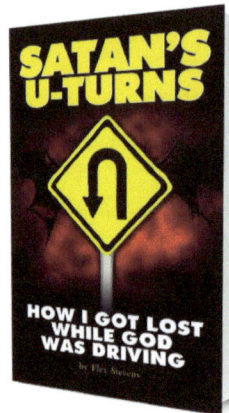

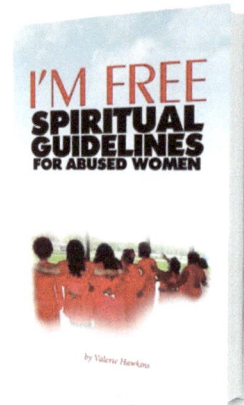

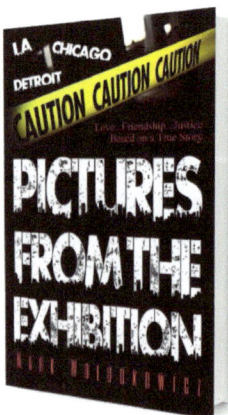

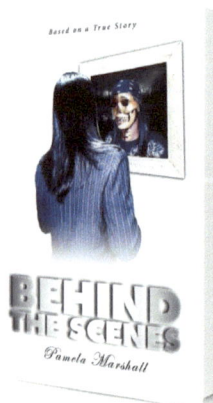

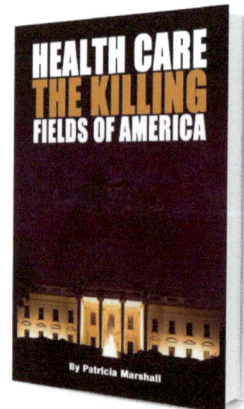

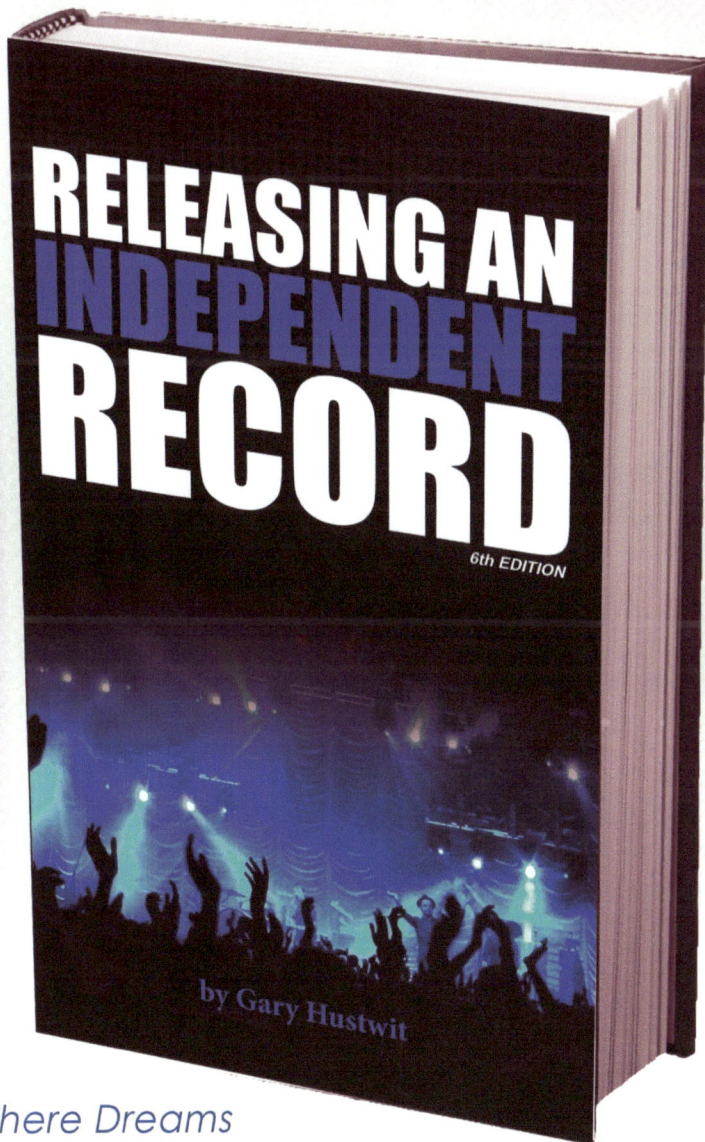

LOOKING FOR A NEW LOOK

LET US CREATE A NEW WEBSITE FOR YOUR COMPANY FOR LESS.

REAL MUSIC. REAL ENTERTAINMENT.®

SDM LIVE

ISSUE 12

Also
PHILLY FAL
7MILE
RADIO
NO'EL
SNYDER
SARAH
APPLEB
LASURIA
"KANDI"
ALLMAN

NEW
KING DILLON
EXCLUSIVE P DOT

CHARLIE B. KEYZ
PUTTING IN MAJOR
LEGWORK IN THE
INDUSTRY

WWW.SDMLIVE.COM

TOYSOULJA
LAGOON
THE NEWEST
MEMBER OF
TEAM MONEY
HUNGRY

ORDER YOUR ISSUE FOR $9.99
Send money order plus $3.95 S&H to: Mocy Publishing, LLC
P.O. 35195 * Detroit, MI 48235

THE ALL NEW STYLE OF MAGAZINE-BOOKS

SDM LIVE ®

www.ingramcontent.com/pod-product-compliance
Lightning Source LLC
Chambersburg PA
CBHW041526070426

42452CB00036B/31